The Autism

KITCHEN

Tricia Ciappelli

Tricia Ciappelli

I have written this book to bring together two worlds. On one side we have a successful Michelin recommended restaurant and on the other is our family kitchen. I have like all parents to a beautiful Autistic child learned how to simply make sure they eat and drink to begin with. Our son Maximus was diagnosed with Autism whilst at pre-school assessment Centre, but we knew before that. There began a journey of being told he may never speak etc and we agreed to focus on believing we have no idea what he can do! We focused on him being happy and healthy which was difficult when at one time he only ate three things.

I have tried to put in recipes for lovely meals that you can adapt to meals for children with sensory issues and sensitivities hopefully you will find some tips and ideas to help you along.

I have a degree in psychology and the more I learn the less I know. We all just do what is best for each of our children. I hope you find this book useful and fun and really hope you enjoy it.

THE BEGINNING

We have come a long way but at the beginning our son ate 3-4 food items and they had to be a certain brand or cooked a certain way exactly. because he was nonverbal up until school he used a picture system called PECS we would take pictures of food and put it in his book on Velcro and if he wanted something he would give us or point to the picture. He now never stops talking but still has a full American accent as he learnt to talk through Echolalia which is a whole book in itself!

Apple chopped, chicken nuggets which had to be the same color with fine breadcrumb, sausages and chips and blackcurrant cordial. This was a huge improvement on baby fruit pouch food and baby rice cakes which was the basics for a couple of years.

We own a restaurant and were lucky enough to travel to my husband's family in Sicily, so our older boy had grown up eating the most amazing food and loved everything from fresh seafood to broccoli! This meant that we were learning as we went with Maximus not only with his Autism but his diet and sensory issues.

Do not stress! Every stage passes and try to be calm and positive. We worked closely with our Doctor, CAHMS and a nutritionist to make sure he was getting the right nutrition.

We supplemented his diet with vitamins and pro biotics. I will seek professional advice on your child's diet especially if they have allergies and like mine a very easily upset tummy.

A lot of Autistic children suffer with gut issues and there is a lot of evidence to support the link between the brain and the gut.

Many people believe that gluten free is extremely helpful along with Casein or dairy free.

We did go gluten free for quite a while and still swap out bread etc. for gluten free options.

Again, I would speak to your doctor about what is best as each child is so different. Allergies is also a profoundly serious subject and again particular to each child and can also change at any time. Some children can get temporary allergies which happened to us and we never really got to the bottom of it. Other children have life threatening allergies and, in the restaurant, making sure there is no cross contamination is critical.

In general, we would prepare and still do our own food and bring it with us to any restaurant.

Gluten-free and Dairy free

Gluten-free and dairy-free recipes are becoming increasingly popular and they can be especially beneficial for children with autism. I also use a lot of olive oil in cooking much to my Italian husband's distress! Coconut oil in baking is great but make sure it is liquid first. My Dad hates butter, so I use olive oil in everything I cook for him even cakes. I have put together some everyday recipes specifically gluten free and dairy free and all the recipes in the book can be adapted.

Veggie Burger

1 can of chickpeas

1 cup of grated or mashed cooked carrots

⅓ a cup of finely chopped onions

2 tbsp gluten free flour

1 tsp olive oil

not in the flour

½ cup of oil

Season with garlic and chili if you like

Mash all the ingredients together and make into burgers patties and bake on a lightly oiled baking tray for 15 minutes 2 tblsp water

on 180C

GLUTEN-FREE AND DAIRY FREE

Gluten-free Quiche

Either buy gluten-free pastry or

11/2 cups of gluten free flour

1tsp salt

1tsp Xanthan gum

Filling

1 cup of non-dairy milk

4 eggs

½ cup of non-dairy cheese if you like it

I cup of vegetables or meat chopped that you prefer (again I keep it plain)

Heat oven to 190C

Mix the pastry ingredients in a bowl and shape into a ball. If you have time chill it for an hour. and rollout and place in a flan dish or any oven proof dish you have. Prick with a fork and bake with parchment and something to weigh the middle down such as baking beans but if you do not have it do not worry. It will just be a bit misshapen. Bake until light golden color about 15 minutes and allow to cool

In a bowl mix the eggs, non-dairy cheese and non-dairy milk in a bowl and any other ingredient you like and pour over the pastry base and bake until its set about 30 minutes.

You can make mini ones in a Yorkshire pudding tin for fun.

Gluten-free pasta and tomato sauce

1 packet of gluten-free pasta

4 cups of ripe chopped tomatoes or a tin of chopped tomatoes

1 cup of chopped onions

1 clove of garlic and a bunch of chopped basil to taste

Tomato pastes optional

Fry the onions in a little oil in a saucepan until golden and add the tomatoes and cook gently and low adding a little water and tomato paste as required. After about 20 minutes you can sieve the sauce to make it smooth. It is ready to serve.

Cook the pasta as per the instructions on the packet until al dente. Serve with the sauce through the pasta or separate depending on preference.

Gluten free Macaroni and cheese bake

1 packet of gluten-free elbow macaroni

2 tblsp of gluten-free flour

2 tblsp of olive oil

2 cups of dairy free milk

2 cups grated dairy free cheddar cheese

¼ cup of gluten free breadcrumbs

Cook the macaroni as per instructions and drain and set aside

In a saucepan warm the oil and mix in the flour.

Gradually add the milk and whisk until thickens and add the cheese. Stir in the pasta and pour into a baking dish. Top with breadcrumbs and pop into the oven on 190C and cook for 25 minutes until golden brown.

A roast dinner for the family is a nice easy meal and all the ingredients can be used to make a shepherd's pie before or use the leftovers. Just remember how you need to chop up the beef or lamb in tiny pieces. My mum and Dad had an old-fashioned mincer that you could attach to the table it was brilliant!

Gluten free and dairy free Shepherd's pie

2 pounds potatoes peeled and chopped

2 tblsp of oil

¼ cup of dairy- free milk

1 carrot finely chopped

2 stalks of celery finely chopped

1 pound of ground, lamb, beef or Quorn

2 tblsp gluten-free flour

2 cups of meat or vegetable stock

Preheat oven to 190C

Boil the potatoes in salted water until soft and drain and mash with the oil and dairy free milk.

In a large frying pan fry the mince, carrot and celery until golden and add the flour and cook until absorbed.

Add the stock and cook through. Transfer to a baking dish and top with the mash and bake in the oven for 25 minutes until top is browning.

This is also good method to make a fish, chicken or vegetable pie

Desserts

Banana pancakes

1 cup of flour

2 bananas

2 eggs

1 tsp. baking powder

1tsp vanilla extract

1 tsp baking powder

1 tablespoon coconut oil

Dairy-free milk if prefer a smoother pancake

Mash the banana until soft and add the rest of the ingredients and mix until a batter consistency.

Heat a pan with a little oil and pour a small amount into the pan and fry for a few minutes and turn until golden on both sides.

You can also add more a little more baking powder, another egg, some sugar to taste and a little dairy free milk and whisk up a giant banana Yorkshire pudding!

COOKIES!

Choc chip gluten free cookies

1 cup of flour

½ tsp baking powder

½ cup of coconut oil

1 cup granulated sugar

1 egg

1 tsp vanilla extract

1 cup dairy free choc chips

Pre heat the oven to 170c

Mix all the ingredients until smooth and then add the choc chips.

Spoon out small pieces of mixture onto baking paper and bake until 10-15.

Apple crumble

4 medium apples

½ cup gluten free flour

½ cup of gluten free oats

½ cup of brown sugar

½ cup coconut oil

1 teaspoon vanilla extract

Heat the oven to 175c

Slice the apples thinly and place in a lightly oiled baking dish

Mix the flour, oats, sugar, oil and extract together in a bowl until crumbly. Spoon over the top of the apples and bake for about 35 minutes until top is golden.

TIPS

You know how your child likes to eat. If they like blue, then get blue plastic plates and lunch boxes. Special cutlery and paper napkins or fun kitchen roll. Shapes can sometimes be as important as texture. Making things into a favorite size or shape can make a huge difference. Adding in a favorite drink bottle or little juice carton can help too. Also keeping foods separate from each other was important for us and thing touching the other did not work so we had lots of little ramekins to make life easier!

Plan meals in advance

Prepare multiple meals on one day at the same time and freeze for easy meals during the week

consider what your child likes and try to make foods they will enjoy
Be open to trying new foods and ingredients

Make mealtimes positive
Encourage your child to help and get involved

Really praise them for trying new foods but at the same time respect their boundaries

I know that this is a hot topic, but I think that it is ok to have fast food now and again.

Priority is food that they will try, and you can build on it. A milkshake can be replicated or added to with yummy ingredients. A child may eat or try a food in a fast food box with fries on the side. We have taken away or fast food on a Saturday night and from that he eats fishfingers, milkshakes, and learned to sit at a very noisy table without ear defenders!

Homemade jellies are great to use some nice juices and I would always and still do put rice cakes in a school bag with an apple. Snacks are not always the bad guys!

Flour, eggs, sugar in a bowl or rolled out with a fruit or chocolate can be fun to make and eat. Have fun and sometimes do not worry about ingredients just experiment!

EATING OUT, TRAVEL AND ALLERGIES

Kitchens and restaurants have lots of noise, smells and that can be overwhelming for our children. Keeping their world small helps. On the table do not be afraid to clear an area for them to play. We had ear defenders, devices, our own food and snacks and toys. We packed heavy but we did get to go places. Although even now Max only likes to go out once a day and we use social stories to prepare him what is happening.

Always ask a restaurant for help they mostly cook from scratch and should be able to help if your child needs gluten free or has allergies

On holiday I brought a suitcase of foods for many years, so I essentially had a packed lunch with me at all times including fruit pouches, rice cakes, foods and snacks and on a flight we would pack presents to unwrap every hour on an 8 hour flight especially. They do not have to be expensive just distractions to eat, drink and play with.

At home we have a well-used trampoline and a quiet space in the house for Maximus to unwind. When we travelled, we bought a little pop up tent and a play tent for the beach and often in the restaurant Max could be found under the table with a book. If the restaurant were more formal, we would make a quick lunch or dinner with treats for him. In Italy like all children they are treated to wonderful VIP treatment and a lot we visited in my husband's home village of Mussomelli in Sicily had a play area in the middle! (Both our boys christening dinners were there!)

Allergies and intolerances

A profoundly serious topic and one that is particular to each child. Hopefully, your child has none but many children with autism suffer from gut issues for many years and their systems always seem to be struggling. Some children have temporary allergies or intolerances which is what happened to us and was not too serious, but Max did do so much better without gluten in his diet although he still has gut issues. All of the recipes can be altered to gluten free or dairy free by simply swapping to gluten free bread and flour etc. It is a personal choice and you will know through trial and error what helps. There is quite a lot of research between the connection between the gut and the brain and new thoughts and research come out all the time but like everything else it is down to the individual child.

Allergies are a different thing completely and you need to work with your doctor directly and take it very seriously. Get help immediately if you think your child has allergies. The hospital can do fantastic noninvasive tests to pinpoint what is causing the reaction and work with you if the need to exclude foods or avoid contact altogether etc. It is important to take steps to keep them safe and healthy. You will become a master at reading labels and will need to work with your nursery or school and your child so everyone is clear on how to manage their allergies or intolerances.

If your child experiences a severe reaction it is important to act quickly. Call 999 if they have difficulty breathing, swelling of the face or tongue, rapid heartbeat, loss of consciousness are medical emergencies and require prompt treatment.

We worked with a nutritionist and various Doctors at the hospital about Max's diet, intolerances and nutrition etc. for many years and I am still learning and adapting as we go. Ask for support and speak to your GP

GREAT
INGREDIENTS
=GREAT FOOD

Great ingredients and plain food

An important lesson I learned in Italy was that if you have just one good ingredient you can make a great dish around it.

We cannot all get to the market, but we can all look at what is in season and fresh and lovely even in the supermarket. We have a little farmers market where I live, and we try to grow as much as we can.

Even growing your own herbs or chili peppers is so good.

A lot of children with Autism like plain food as we know so something like this is not going to work a lot of the time.

You can make a plain pasta and add a little store-bought pesto or chop, basil, garlic, pine nuts and pecorino or Parmesan to taste with a little olive oil and mix through If you like it though.

When you order in a restaurant make sure to ask for no garnish as a lot of chefs do like to do this and the sight of it even if it is removed after is enough to cause a

meltdown.

If your child eats pasta sauce that is amazing as you can blend or mash small amounts of vegetables into it and it is so nutritious. You can even make your own base sauce for pizza by adding in a little blended veg or even carrot juice.

We had to stick to plain stock but some blended vegetables if it was not too noticeable. Meatballs or Veggie balls were good for this.

needs and preferences

Where?

It does not matter. If the table is too noisy, too bright, too many people this may simply be too much of a sensory overload. It is ok and often it passes. The most important thing is food first. My son will often take his food to his bedroom on a tray. He will still come and chat and have a drink before or after. It is all about what makes them comfortable and relaxed

Vegetarian and losing foods

For a while you will feel things are going ok and then you will suddenly loose a food or foods and you have to try and build up again. A slight panic occurs but be calm go back to trust and trust you will get there. Was is now vegetarian of his request and overnight knocked out most foods except chops peas apples and sweets. Jed went back to trying veggie sausage, veggie roast, fish fingers potatoes and jacket potatoes so it's not too bad!

WALKING AND
FORAGING

One of the best things we did was simply going for a walk with a purpose.

Blackberry picking, mushroom picking, fishing, collecting wild garlic. These are things we do all year around which not only makes wonderful memories but really helps to encourage positive interaction with food. It was very short walks in the beginning and I never went alone in case we had any problems but now we literally walk for miles. I know it's hard if you live in a city but even a walk to a little market nice and early when it's quiet can be lovely.

Broccoli and Seabass

My oldest boy loved broccoli. We used to cook them whole and give him a knive and fork to cut down his trees. I recall a night in a restaurant in Sicily and large group of very smart older gentlemen were having a seafood banquet and they saw the way little Alexander was enjoying his sea bass in his highchair and sent over all the best fish for him to eat. Which he did! He would and still does love and try all cuisines and has a passion for food. I don't know if Max will ever eat a whole sea bass or cut down a broccoli tree but he makes and eats a great pizza (without sauce) which I never dreamed he would do! Remember your child is on their own food journey and that they are all different.

There are problems with this as children have incredibley good palets and can taste and feel if you have tried to hide a crushed iron tablet etc. It is also hard to monitor what they have had and you can put them off a food they love and loose their trust. That said if you can put a tiny bit of carrot juice in a banana smoothie and go undetected it is a win win. If could find a way to get a little extra healthy in a cake, juice, jelly or even a pizza I would always try. Just a little as the best way is always in plain sight but I still may add a little vitamin juice to a milkshake when I can!

Making more out of your ingredients

Because we must often cook slightly different meals it can work out expensive and in these current times, we all must make things go further. The best way is to bulk up the protein with vegetables or carbohydrates.

1 PACK OF MINCE = 3 MEALS!

For example, you can make a packet of mince or veggie mince do three meals

Divide the mince or veggie mince into three

Make the meatballs from my recipe but add in more breadcrumb and egg to bulk it out. Do the same with the Bolognese but add in more vegetables. Use the last portion of mince as a chili sauce with kidney beans, onion and chili and tomato sauce or I would make for Max a Sheppard's pie with nothing except veggie mince and gravy and mash. Another option is cook mince and add extra mash and make mini pasties with store bought puff pastry for quickness.

It is sometimes good to have a baking day even if it is once a week and you can stock the freezer with a few things.

Also, if you are ever roasting a chicken always boil up the bones for stock and freeze it can be used as a base for so many things

So, add vegetables, breadcrumb, potatoes and get baking to get things
to go further.

HOLIDAYS

They are a good time to try new foods. Putting things out buffet style and giving them a fun plate to try when they feel hungry. Even if it is to touch or smell only. It took years of Christmas for Max to try something new. One year my Mum was cooking turkey and he seemed to like the smell. She asked him would you like to try a Christmas chicken and handed him a plate with the white small pieces and some juice. We all could not look! He came back empty handed for more. We were overjoyed he had a new healthy food for the first time in years. Fast forward to now he is vegetarian, but he still loves a vegetarian roast and gravy.

Mario's Meatballs

INGREDIENTS

1-pound (450g) ground beef and pork

1 egg

½ cup Parmigiano Reggiano, grated

½ cup breadcrumbs

3 tbsps. milk 3
tbsps. olive oil

1 Tin chopped tomatoes or 3
cups of fresh

Directions

Put meat, an egg, Parmigiano
Reggiano and milk in a bowl.

Heat olive oil in a frying pan. Cook
the meatballs until golden brown. Add
crushed whole tomatoes and cook over
low heat for 15 minutes. I keep the
meatballs without sauce for the
children

BREADBALLS

2 cups of breadcrumbs
1 and half cups of grated pecorino
2 eggs

You also cook courgette and take the
skin off and finely chop and make
courgette balls

Potatoes

JACKET POTATOES

microwave or cook in bulk in the oven when you have other things in or Microwave for 5 minutes and wrap in foil and pop in the oven for 5 -10 minutes on 180 c.

CHIPS

oven chips are the easiest and even have microwave chips in the freezer in case. If you want to make fresh and have an air fryer that is great, but I would stay away from deep fat frying if you can and maybe shallow fry some in a pan.

GOLDEN POTATOES

pre boil some potatoes for about 15 minutes

dry them and chop them to a size smaller slightly than roast potatoes and shallow fry until golden and crunchy. Do not keep turning them and they will go crunchy and golden.

MASH

Potatoes, butter and cream
Potatoes, olive oil and milk

Microwave store bought if a child likes the square shape is ok and saves time as you can just microwave

CROQUETTES

Make a sausage shape with mash roll in flour and dip in egg and breadcrumb and fry for about 4 minutes

GNOCCHI

- ◆ 2 potatoes, peeled
- ◆ 2 cups all-purpose flour 1
- ◆ egg

mash the potatoes and the ingredients together

toll out into sausages and cut into little pieces approx. 1 inch

cook in salted boiling water after for about 3 minutes

POTATOE AND COURGETTE BALLS

take mash or chopped boiled potatoes and cooked courgette chopped (take off the green outside!

Mix into flat small Pattie's and either bake in the oven with a little oil or shallow fry

Chicken in Breadcrumbs

You can either make nuggets, burgers or whole

breasts but I always flatten them out, so they are thin, so you do not have to cook them too long and

they do not go too brown.

INGREDIENTS

Chicken breast
1-2eggs Sprinkle
of flour

DIRECTIONS

- Pound chicken to flatten I also sprinkle with flour
- Sprinkle salt and pepper on each.
- Dip into beaten eggs and then coat with breadcrumbs.
- In a large pan, heat oil over medium heat.
- Place chicken in the frying pan and brown on both sides, cooking about 5 minutes on each side, or until chicken is fork tender.
- Cooking time will vary depending on how thick your chicken is.

Pasta

- In Sicily some of the pasta that the children eat at lunch is exceptionally light, almost like a soup with pasta in it. This was a great idea I modified for us as I would often cook plain pasta in a chicken stock or light seafood stock and serve plain and almost dry.

• PASTA AL FORNO

- cups of Bolognese sauce
- 1 pack of penne pasta
- 1 cup of peas

- 3boiled eggs
- 1packet of sliced ham or chopped up fresh gammon ham or pancetta
- 1 cup of mozzarella
- Half a cup of Parmesan

• Directions

- Cook the penne pasta as per instructions and drain. Add the Bolognese sauce, peas and ham Place in a large baking dish and add the boiled eggs sliced in half. Top with cheese and bake in a preheated oven for twenty minutes at 180 c

PASTA ALLA NORMA

- 1 Aubergine
- 1 clove of garlic
- 1 ton of Passata or chopped tomatoes or fresh tomatoes
- 1 teaspoon dried oregano
- 1/4 teaspoon red pepper flakes 2 tablespoons tomato paste
- 1 packet of pasta such as rigatoni
- Handful fresh small basil

DIRECTIONS

Aubergines can either be sliced and roasted in advance or sliced and put into salt water to soak for an hour or so. Take out and dry and chop into chunks. Gently fry and add the rest of the ingredients and cook on low for about an hour.

Cook pasta as normal and serve with either Parmesan or Pecorino cheese. If you have extra aubergine take of the black skin and mash mix with egg and breadcrumb and fry in Pattie's for a nice starter or snack

Ravioli for you and me

WITH RICOTTA IN LEMON PARSLEY BUTTER

INGREDIENTS

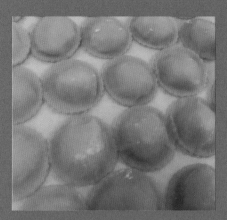

Filling

1 and a half cups of ricotta cheese Half a cup of Parmesan

1 Lemon juiced and zested

1egg

Parsley

Mix in a bowl till it comes to get and divide in small portions as you place in the pasta pockets

PASTA

3 eggs

2 cups of flour

1 tbsp. olive oil

1. Mix the eggs and oil and a little water together and pour into the flour and mix
2. Roll out and use whatever is handy to cut out shapes e.g. an egg cup.
3. Put a little filling in the middle and top with another circle and squeeze out the air. you can use a little water to seal.
4. Cook in boiling water for 3 minutes and serve with a little butter and parsley.

Max's Ravioli

We would either put nothing in it except mozzarella and have it with Parmesan or we tried a little sausage meat but often plain and dry was a favorite with olive oil and Parmesan on top.

Seafood

COD

Adapting meals from your own delicious meals can be done easily if you think ahead

COD FILLET WITH TOMATO AND BASIL CRUST ON A BED OF SPINACH

Ingredients

Cod fillet

Bag of fresh spinach or frozen

Half a cup of breadcrumbs

A few large tomatoes

Olive oil, garlic pesto

1. Wilt the spinach in a frying pan with a little water, salt pepper and olive oil
2. Add breadcrumbs to a bowl, add chopped tomatoes, olive oil, basil and garlic.
3. Pre heat the oven to 160-180c
4. Place the cod in a baking dish and sprinkle the breadcrumb mixture over the top
5. Bake for about 15 minutes until golden
6. serve on the bed of spinach with fresh basil or pesto garnish

FISH BALLS

Ingredients

Cod fillet

Half a cup of breadcrumbs
Flour

1 egg

1. Cook the fish with your own with a little olive oil
2. Cool and break it up into a bowl and add breadcrumb a little milk or an egg and form with flour into balls.
3. Lightly fry in a shallow pan until just golden brown

BOLOGNESE

- tbsp olive oil

- 1 onion, finely chopped

- 1 carrot, peeled, finely chopped

- 1 celery stick, trimmed, finely chopped
- 500g beef mince you can do half pork mince

- 1/3 cup tomato paste

- 2 x 400g cans diced tomatoes 1
- tsp oregano leaves

- 1/2 cup water

- 500g thin spaghetti

- Parmesan cheese, shaved, to serve

1 tablespoon of the oil in a frypan over medium heat.

Add onions and cook until they start to soften, without browning (6   Add the meat and brown

Then the remaining ingredients and stir Simmer over lowest heat for half an hour but the longer the richer the taste

With this sauce you can make traditional Pasta or Lasagne

if you do not add the tomatoes you can make a Sheppard's pie, mince and potatoes even mini pasties!

When we are in Sicily, we eat a lot of dishes like this and long long lunches are a big part of family life! Just by being exposed to all these wonderful foods Maximus tried breadsticks and cheese for the first time although I think it was because they came in bright packets, but it was two new things which at the time was amazing. We still always packed our own dinner for him, but he could try anything he wanted, and we always made sure there was something we knew he would like. If you find your child is going off some foods at home, it is worth a try putting out a little mixed plate of their own with some things they like and some they have not tried. Never force food onto your child always encourage and try to keep it positive and fun. I know it is so hard when you are worried about their diet but just keep trying! When a child loses a food, it is so worrying when they only eat a few things. I remember rushing one day and overcooking a pancake. I tried to hide the slightly burnt bit thinking it would be fine, but he did not eat it and it also put him off pancakes for months. At the time it was a big setback and I felt awful. This is all part of sensory processing disorder and Autism. We describe it to him as his superpower. He can smell better, taste better and hear better than others. Like a superhero can hear things better or like a cat can see better in the dark or a dog can smell better than humans. This was just how we described things to him when he was little and he had to wear ear defenders in noisy places and couldn't stand strong smells and would run out of the kitchen if I even attempted to cook a curry. We did eventually get him to try store-bought mini pancakes months later and he now makes his own pancakes!

24

Alexander's
student noodles

Ingredients

- 8 oz of noodles
- 1 egg per person
- 3 spring onions
- 4 cups of chicken or vegetable stock
- Sesame oil to taste
- Chopped chili to taste
- Chicken, prawn or Tofu

Directions

1. Heat the stock and add the soy
2. Cook the chicken, prawn or Tofu in a little oil in a wok and set aside
3. Add the egg the middle of the stock and take pot of the heat so the egg poaches. Add the noodles and peas chicken, prawn or tofu
4. Garnish with chopped spring onions and chili, soy sauce and sesame oil

Happy noodles

Ingredients

4 oz noodles

2 cups of stock

Simply heat the stock and add the noodles and cook as per instructions depending if they are fresh or dried.

For many years we would have to drain them but over the years we built up the stock he would have and put things in little bowls in the side he could add like sweet corn or peas. it was a slow process. Salt and pepper are personal taste.

Ice lollies, Smoothies and Drinks

Most of the smoothie recipes can be made into ice lollies. If you do not have time it is fine to buy juices and make combinations to try drinks that can be a healthy addition for your child's diet. Sometimes the colors do not look so good although they taste so it is a good opportunity to use a drink bottle that is covered up. Max liked ice so I would often use ice and even recycle covered plastic drinks bottles if he liked using them.

SMOOTHIES

STRAWBERRY AND BANANA SMOOTHIE

1 cup of frozen strawberries 1 Banana

1 cup of milk or milk substitute 1 TBLS honey

Pop all the ingredients in a blender and blend until smooth

BLUEBERRY AND MANGO

1 cup of frozen blueberry 1 cup of frozen mango

1 cup of coconut water 1 TBLS Honey

ORANGE AND APPLE

1 cup of orange juice 1 cup of apple juice

Half a cup of spinach or store-bought green juice 1 cup of ice

A dash of blackcurrant cordial

MILKSHAKES

Mix all the ingredients in a blender and blend until smooth

if you do not have a blender simply use juice
and milks and stir with some ice

MANGO AND CARROT MILKSHAKE

1 cup of frozen
mango Half a
cup of carrots

1 cup big unsweetened
coconut milk Half a cup
of ice

STRAWBERRY AND SPINACH

Half a cup of frozen
strawberries Half a cup
of spinach

1 cup of
almond milk
Half a cup of
ice

BLUEBERRY AND KALE

1 cup of frozen
blueberries Half a
cup of Kale

1 cup of unsweetened almond milk

Half a cup of ice them and chop them to a size
smaller slightly than roast potatoes and
shallow fry until golden and crunchy. Do not
keep turning them and they will go crunchy
and golden.

Slushies and lollies

Blend fresh fruit ingredients in a blender

and freeze in molds

If you do not have a blender use any fresh or carton juice that your child likes

STRAWBERRY YOGURT LOLLY

1 cup of frozen strawberries

1 cup of yogurt

1 tbsp honey

WATERMELON AND ORANGE JUICE

Blend the watermelon and mix with orange juice simply mix and pour to freeze

RASPBERRY LEMONADE LOLLY

1 cup of frozen raspberries 1 cup of lemonade

1 tbsp of honey

Seafood
DOVER SOLE ON THE BONE

Ingredients

Dover sole

I Lemon

1 Tblsp of
olive oil

1. place the fish on a flat dish with olive oil or butter
2. Pre heat the oven to180c
3. Bake for about 15 minutes until golden

CALAMARI RINGS

Ingredients

1/2 cup cornstarch 1/2
cup flour

1 1/2 teaspoon baking powder 3/4
teaspoon salt

1 dash sugar
1/2 cup milk
1/3 cup water

1. Mix all the ingredients in a bowl
2. Dip the calamari ring in the batter mix
3. Lightly fry in oil until just golden brown

ONE GOOD THING

An important lesson I learned in Italy was that if you have just one good ingredient you can make a great dish around it.

We cannot all get to the market, but we can all look at what is in season and fresh and lovely even in the supermarket. We have a little farmers market where I live, and we try to grow as much as we can.

Even growing your own herbs or chili peppers is so good.

MUSHROOM RISOTTO

1 packet of risotto rice

4 cups of chicken or vegetable stock
Half a cup of Parmesan

Half a cup of wine if for adults!

2 cup of chopped mushrooms 1
cup of chopped onions

Fry the onions and mushrooms and onions in oil add the rice and cook for further 5 minutes. Warm the stock in a separate pan and put the stock in gradually and reduce down for approx. 25 minutes continuously adding stock when the rice is cooked and creamy add in the Parmesan and add truffle oil to taste served topped with Parmesan

SOUPS

If you child eats soup that is amazing, I struggled for many years to get Maximus to try any until last week and he had some outside in a cup on a cold day. I think it helps when they see other people eating things.

I love soup and the smell of the ham and vegetable soup cooking on the stove is the best.

I used some of our leftover soups as a base to put in a pasta sauce or mix in with his vegetables. Always make a stock from a roast chicken or ham. You can always freeze it and use it for so many things.

TOMATO SOUP

1 Onion

Basil and oregano to taste and cream to garnish

3 cloves of garlic

4 cups of chicken or vegetable broth

4 cups of tomatoes or two tins of tinned chopped tomatoes

Chop the onions and gently fry in a large pan and then chop and add the tomatoes and cook until soft.

Lastly add the broth and cook on a low heat, covered for a further 20 minutes. Blend the ingredients or mash and serve.

MINESTRONE

1 cup of potatoes and seasonal vegetables peeled and chopped

Half a cup of Haricot beans

1 onion chopped

1 stick of celery chopped

4 cups of chicken or vegetable stock

Half a cup of pasting pasta if desired

2 tomatoes chopped

Simply put all the ingredients except the pasta in a large pot and bring to boil then reduce heat and simmer for 25 minutes and add the mini pasta later as per instructions on the packet.

MUM 'S BIG HAM SOUP

1 Ham shank on the bone boil first for 1 hour then drain then set aside. Cut of the fat

Half a cup of red lentils washed in cold water

1 potato

1onion

2 carrots

1 stick of celery

4 cups of vegetable or chicken stock

Bring to boil and then simmer for an hour

remove the ham and take of the meat and place in the soup add more stock or water to taste and cook for a further 30 minutes

From Sicily

We found many dishes whilst in Sicily and some such as Panelle are a day to day staple. The rule is fresh and simple. I love how each ingredient is celebrated. If you can encourage your child to help prepare, touch, peel and chop it is so positive. They may not eat any of it but one day they may try a bit and worst case it helps them to experience new smells and flavors without getting too overwhelmed

ALMOND BISCUITS

500g almond meal

6 egg whites, beaten until stiff

300g white sugar

1 tsp vanilla essence

1 tsp almond essence

Icing sugar and almonds to coat the biscuits

Beat the egg whites together until stiff

Mix in a bowl and rest for 1/2 an hour. Preheat oven to 180C.

Make small sausage shapes and use a fork to make tracks across them

Dip in a little egg white and coat with almonds

Place on a lightly oiled baking tray and cook at 180c for 10-15 minutes

PANELLE

We eat these as savory snacks and without parsley they are a firm favorite with the children

INGREDIENTS

* 400g of chickpea flour

* 2 tbsp of parsley,
* chopped salt and water until it is a paste

* vegetable oil, for deep-frying

Mix all the ingredients together in a pan and heat up until thickened.

Spread on a grease proof tray or baking sheet and place in the fridge to cool.

when set slice into into squares and triangles about the size of you were cutting a slice of bread into four.

then simply fry. I deep fry in a small pot until golden. You can serve plain or with lemon juice

Everyday meals

You can cook a standard meal of a meat, vegetables and potatoes and adapt any of those ingredients for your child if they do not like it the traditional way. We would also eat a lot of things originally, we started cooking for Max.

I would take pork or steak and make it into schnitzels with store bought Panko crumbs and then cut them into a strong shapes such as a triangle, square or circle and if he had leftovers they were always popular with the rest of the family.

Frying or roasting aubergines is something I do often for various dishes and I always keep some and remove the skin. When chopped you can make vegetarian balls for pasta or add to other dishes.

If you make homemade Pizza make some chocolate pizza with Nutella chocolate.

The children love cooking this one!

Desserts

Whatever is your child's favorite fruit or sweet thing go with it!

This plate is too busy for my son I would put the ice cream in a separate bowl or cone and fruit in a ramekin and the cake or pie in a bowl

MERINGUE
4 egg whites

Pinch of salt

1 cup (220g) caster sugar,

1/2 tsp vanilla essence

Simply whip the egg whites until stiff and add the caster sugar a spoon at a time and fold in as you go

- Drop out a large spoonful of the mix onto a baking sheet
- Cook on a low heat such as 120c for about 1 and a half hours and then leave to cool

This recipe is great to add variations as it is a good base. In the recipe below I would not use sesame seeds for Max as he just liked things plain You can also add in Lemon or orange zest or replace 1 of the cups of flour with ground almonds. Lots of experimenting to be done!

Sesame Cookies

1 cup of flour

1/2 cup of butter

¾ cup of sugar

1 tsp baking powder

¼ tsp salt

1 tsp vanilla extract

2 eggs
1 cup of toasted sesame seeds

Heat the oven to 180C

Mix all the ingredients in a bowl and form into a dough ball

Make into cookie shapes

Cover in sesame seeds and place in the oven on a baking sheet for 25 minutes

CHOCOLATE

When I told Maximus, I was writing a cookbook for families like ours he wanted to join in his suggestion was chocolate and it is actually a good idea! Melt some chocolate and put into some shapes add a stick for chocolate pops etc. it is just about involving your child with food prep making what works for them and have fun!!!

LITTLE CHEFS

Anything you can mix in a bowl is usually fun. We make pastry and pizza and of course little sponge cakes.

Box cakes are ok if your child likes them it is more about your child getting involved with food and having fun!

EASY CAKES

Ingredients

2 cups of flour
3/4 cup of sugar

125g of butter or olive oil
1 cup of milk

A little vanilla or chocolate powder if they like the taste.

1. Pop everything in a bowl and mix how they like hands or forks.
2. Divide into cases or make a mini cake
3. Cook on 160 for about 10 minutes

DAD'S FUNNY EGG

2 -3 eggs per person
Sliced bread

Milk
Olive Oil

Use any bread you have and break it up into chunks

Mix the eggs in a bowl with a little milk
Add in the bread and let it soak up the mixture.

Heat a frying pan with oil and pour the mixture in and cook on one side and turn when golden. Do not worry if it breaks that is what

makes it funny.

For Max I would use breadcrumbs instead and cook on a low heat or even in the oven, so it was all the same color and shape.

RICOTTA AND EGG

1 cup of ricotta

2 eggs
Breadcrumbs
Milk

Olive oil

So simple to make just mix the ingredients in a bowl and shallow fry like and omelette

I would also adapt this with more breadcrumbs to make vegetarian ricotta balls that you can serve plain or with a tomato and basil sauce

The picture was a Max experiment ! I really hope you enjoyed this cookbook and the recipes and tips made the challenges that we face a little bit easier. Remember to be patient and do not worry if a recipe does not work out first time. Keep experimenting, try new things and most importantly enjoy!

BBQ

These are a big part of our summer and I we keep things simple. Bread, meat and or fish and a salad. Light the BBQ and go. The problem is that for autistic children it can be too strong tasting or has bits on it.

We found the easiest way to get around this was to prepare in advance. So, a sausage, hotdog, chips or whatever it is cooked as the like it and then popped into a foil parcel and warmed up on the BBQ.

These parcels are a great way to cook fish just add in olive oil and lemon juice and fresh herbs.

If there are a few people, we would often have the pop-up tent around so there was always somewhere quiet.

Also try to relax and have a packed lunch on standby in case the BBQ is late, or routine is moved around!

Everyone is finding it harder to budget now but beautiful food can still be made for you and your family. Dishes with Potatoes, eggs, flour, pasta and rice are great to mix such as the soufflé above is made from basic ingredients and the children can have the same or cheese on toast or cheese and potato balls.The fish or meat can be used to make dinner and keep some back for a soup or pasta sauce for lunch or dinner the next

day.

Times are changing again and it is becoming cheaper to cook from scratch than buy convenience so get making those pancakes for

breakfast!

I live on the Isle of Man. It is a small island in the middle of the Irish Sea. We are lucky to have amazing local ingredients on our doorstep and I will always try to adapt something for Maximus if I can. Even Lobster! If you take some of the meat and finely chop it it can be added to mash to make Lobster Croquettes. I will sometimes buy ready made Panko breadcrumbs as they seemed to make things more appealing for the children. It is always worth trying and although I agree that most of the times I failed it is worth it for those rare moments of success!

These apples were given to us and all our neighbors by some of our neighbours children from the tree in their garden. We made the gluten-free apple crumble recipe from this book!

It also reminded me that Max to this day will only eat pink lady apples and he must use an apple slicer and corer to section it. He first ate an apple by watching me prepare some cooking apples and copied me! It did take many years though!!!

My family is everything to me xxxMary and Charlie (Mum and Dad) Alexander aka Mr Handsome (our oldest son), Mario (My husband) and of course Maximus! I love them all so much and I am so lucky to have them in my life.

ORTOFINO

Tricia Ciappelli